MY NAME IS JIMMY CARTER

MY NAME IS JIMMY CARTER

By June Behrens

Pictures by
Marjorie Burgeson

11,716

A GOLDEN GATE JUNIOR BOOK

Childrens Press, Chicago

Library of Congress Cataloging in Publication Data

Behrens, June.
  My name is Jimmy Carter.

  "A Golden Gate junior book."
  SUMMARY: A brief biography of the Georgia peanut
farmer who became the thirty-ninth President.
  1. Carter, Jimmy, 1924-   —Juvenile literature.
2. Presidents—United States—Biography—Juvenile
literature. [1. Carter, Jimmy, 1924 -   2. Presidents]
I. Burgeson, Marjorie. II. Title.
E873.B44   973.926'092'4 [B]   77-16648
ISBN 0-516-08754-1

The White House

One cold day in January, 1977, a man named Jimmy Carter walked down the middle of a street in the nation's capital, Washington, D.C. Walking beside him were his wife, Rosalynn, and their nine-year-old daughter, Amy. They were walking to the White House where they were going to live. Jimmy Carter had just been made the 39th President of the United States.

The people on the sidewalks waved and cheered. The new President smiled and waved back.

Jimmy Carter and his family moved into their new home. Mrs. Carter is called the First Lady. Amy Carter enrolled in a school a few blocks from the White House. Boys and girls from many countries go to that school.

The Carter family came from Georgia. Their old home is a peanut farm near a little town called Plains.

Whenever they can, the President and his family visit Plains. Mr. Carter's mother, who is known as Miss Lillian, lives in Plains. His sisters, brother and cousins live there too.

Mr. Carter likes to walk in the fields where he worked as a boy. Jimmy Carter was born and raised here. His people have lived in this part of the country for over 150 years.

When Jimmy was still a very young boy, he helped his father with the farm work. He carried water and pulled weeds when he was only six years old. When he was older he helped with the field plowing. Jimmy's father taught him that it was very important to work hard and to always do one's best.

Jimmy found plenty of time to play with other boys and girls. He was known as the best tree-climber in the neighborhood. One summer he and his friends built a tree house. They often slept there overnight. They hunted for arrowheads in the fields. They built dams across the creek. They caught catfish and eels. They cooked their fish over a campfire.

Jimmy was a sandy-haired boy with freckles and hazel-blue eyes. In school his teacher, Miss Julia Coleman, knew he was a good worker. She gave him many books to read.

Some of the books were long and had hard words. But Jimmy read them all very carefully. He knew it was important to learn about many different things.

In school Jimmy was a School Boy
Patrolman. He wore a white belt and
a tin badge. He helped to enforce
the school safety rules. Part of his job
was to go for help when the old
school bus broke down.

In high school Jimmy played
basketball. He always played to win.
If his team lost a game, he tried
harder than ever to win next time.

When Jimmy was still a young boy he decided that he wanted to go to the United States Naval Academy when he was old enough. The Academy is in Annapolis, Maryland. It is a college where young people learn to be officers in the U.S. Navy.

Jimmy entered the Academy when he was 19. He graduated after three years.

The year of his graduation he married Rosalynn Smith. Rosalynn had grown up in Plains too.

21

Jimmy was an officer in the Navy for seven years. He served on battleships and submarines. Sometimes he had frightening experiences. He remembers the time he was on a submarine in the Pacific Ocean. A giant wave almost washed him overboard.

Jimmy Carter left the Navy when his father died. He knew he was needed back home in Plains. He took over the family peanut farming business.

Jimmy was a good farmer and businessman. He worked from sunrise to sunset. His peanut business grew.

But most of all he wanted to help the people of his state, both white folks and black.

He was elected to
the Georgia State Senate. As a state
senator he served the people for four
years.

After two terms in the Senate,
Jimmy worked as a leader in his
community. On Sundays he taught
Sunday School in the Plains Baptist
Church.

Jimmy Carter was sure he could do a good job for his state as its Governor. Thousands of people in Georgia, both black and white, thought so too. They voted for Jimmy. He was elected Governor of Georgia in 1970.

One day his mother asked him, "Jimmy, what are you going to do when you're not Governor any more?" Jimmy answered, "Moma, I'm going to run for President of the United States—and I'm going to win."

Jimmy Carter knew that to be elected President he would have to work very hard. He would have to meet people all over the country. He would have to let them know his ideas and tell them what kind of President he wanted to be.

So he and Rosalynn traveled from coast to coast, to nearly every state in the Union. Jimmy talked to thousands of people—in shopping centers, in factories, in churches. He said, "My name is Jimmy Carter. I want to be your President."

Jimmy talked and the people listened. More and more people liked what they heard.

When it came time for the people to vote, in November, 1976, they elected Jimmy Carter their leader, the 39th President of the United States of America.

JIMMY CARTER
James Earl Carter, Jr.

1924   October 1. Born near Plains, Georgia

1941   Graduated from Plains High School

1941   Attended Georgia Southwestern College, Americus, Georgia

1942   Attended Georgia Institute of Technology, Atlanta, Georgia

1943   Entered U.S. Naval Academy at Annapolis

1946   Graduated from U.S. Naval Academy

1946   Married Rosalynn Smith

1946-1953
  Served as an officer on battleships and submarines

1951   A senior officer on the *Seawolf,* one of the first atomic submarines

1953   Death of James Earl Carter, Sr.

1953   Resigned from the Navy
  Returned to Plains

1955-1962
  Chairman of Sumpter County Board of Education

1962-1966
  Georgia State Senator

1970   Elected Govenor of Georgia

1974   Declared as a candidate for Presidential nomination

1976   Elected President of the United States

1977   January 20 Inaugurated as 39th President of the United States

One cold day in January, 1977, a man walked down the middle of a street in the nation's capital, Washington, D.C. Beside him were his wife and small daughter. They were walking to the White House where they were going to live. The man's name was Jimmy Carter and he had just been made the 39th President of the United States.

Specially written for primary age children, here is the story of Jimmy Carter, from his boyhood days when he helped his father on the Carter farm near Plains, Georgia, to the first days of his Presidency. We see him as a freckle-faced youngster who not only worked hard but found time to play with his friends—climbing trees, building a tree house, fishing the creek for catfish. We see him at school, mastering the difficult books his teacher gave him. We see him as a cadet at Annapolis, then as an officer in the U.S. Navy. We follow his later career in Georgia as he serves his state as a state senator, then as governor. The book comes to an exciting climax as Jimmy Carter, the little-known candidate, takes to the campaign trail to win the Presidency of the United States. The delightful full-color illustrations greatly enhance this very readable book.

JUNE BEHRENS has a rich background of knowledge and experience in dealing with the reading capabilities of primary age children. For many years a reading specialist in one of California's largest public school systems, she has also written a score of books for youngest readers covering an astonishing range of subjects—from appreciating art to mastering the metric system. A graduate of the University of California at Santa Barbara, she holds a Credential in Early Childhood Education and has a Master's degree in Administration from the University of Southern California. With her husband, a well-known educator, she spends vacations abroad visiting such widely separated places as Hong Kong and South Africa.

MARJORIE BURGESON not only illustrates children's books but is a painter, sculptor, graphics designer and designer of toys as well. Her work has been exhibited in many galleries and art museums and she has won a number of awards and prizes. She is a graduate of California's Scripps College and holds the degree of Master of Fine Arts from Claremont Graduate School. She and her husband have two daughters and live in Claremont. Mrs. Burgeson has illustrated four previous books for Childrens Press—*The First Day of School, The Valentine Box, The Halloween Witch* and *The Christmas Magic-Wagon.*